CHARLES CANTALUPO

Where War Was

Poems and Translations from Eritrea

Images by
LAWRENCE F. SYKES

MKUKI NA NYOTA
DAR—ES—SALAAM

PUBLISHED BY
Mkuki na Nyota Publishers Ltd
P. O. Box 4246
Dar es Salaam, Tanzania
www.mkukinanyota.com

© Charles Cantalupo et al, 2016

ISBN 978-9987-753-61-1

Visit www.mkukinanyota.com to read more about and to purchase any of Mkuki na Nyota books. You will also find featured authors, interviews and news about other publisher/author events. Sign up for our e-newsletters for updates on new releases and other announcements.

Distributed world wide outside Africa by African Books Collective.
www.africanbookscollective.com

CONTENTS

Preface   5

POEMS

TRANSLATIONS OF POEMS

I began writing about Eritrea in the summer of 1995. I have continued to visit and to write about it ever since. The last two thirds of my memoir, *Joining Africa—from Anthills to Asmara,* tracks the course of this work until 2005.

Where War Was includes my poems and translations of poems by Eritreans from the same years but also from the last decade, too.

The Eritrean poet, Reesom Haile, and I published collections of his poems in 2000 and 2002: *We Have Our Voice* and *We Invented the Wheel,* respectively. *Where War Was* contains translations of poems by Reesom Haile that we worked on before his death in 2003, which we never finished or published and that I have returned to working on since then.

Where War Was also includes translations of poems by other Eritrean poets. I first heard two of these poems—"Under the Sycamores" by Zeineb Yassin and "War and a Woman" by Saba Kidane—in 2000 at the international conference and festival that I co-chaired, called "Against All Odds: African Languages and Literatures into the 21st Century," which took place in Asmara, Eritrea. The eponymous 2007 documentary that I wrote and directed about the conference included both Zeineb Yassin and Saba Kidane performing their poems. Dessale Berekeht and I translated "Under the Sycamores," and Ghirmai Negash and I translated "War and a Woman." Both translations appear in subtitles in the film. Negash and I included "War and a Woman" and additional poems by Kidane in an anthology we both edited and translated—titled *Who Needs a Story: Contemporary Eritrean Poetry in Tigrinya, Tigre and Arabic* published in 2005. I also discussed Saba Kidane's and Reesom Haile's poems in my book about the poems in *Who Needs a Story,* titled *War and Peace in Contemporary Eritrean Poetry,* published in 2009.

In 2008, Ghirmai Negash and I translated, performed, and published a selection of traditional, Eritrean oral poetry including "What Can I Call You?," "Our State," and "Son and Father." In *Who Needs a Story* three years before, we decided, as we stated in the introduction, "to include only written poetry and not Eritrean oral poetry, which ha[d] a long and rich tradition, and which . . . [wa]s still very important and pervasive in Eritrea." At the same time, we affirm[ed] that "[w]e firmly believed that the depth, breadth, and high quality of Eritrean oral poetry warrant[ed] a translation project and an edition on its own." Our translations of these poems included in *Where War Was* are the beginning of such a project.

Like the translations, my poems in *Where War Was* range over two decades. I had been traveling to Africa—including Egypt, West and East Africa—and writing poetry about it for ten years before my first visit to Eritrea in 1995 when I wrote the title poem, "Where War Was." Moreover, while I was traveling as a kind of literary pilgrim, I also wanted to witness the site of one of Africa's greatest, harshest, and most recent revolutions for independence: Eritrea's thirty-year armed struggle—the longest war in modern African history—to liberate itself from Ethiopian colonial rule, added on to Eritrea's seventy-year struggle before that to liberate itself first from Italian and then from British colonial rule. I saw plenty of evidence of war: from the unrepaired bullet holes in the newly painted stucco buildings' walls to the near legions of amputees and veterans—*tegedelti*—in elaborately constructed wheel chairs; from the vast graveyard of tanks and other armaments with a variety of nations' emblems to the veterans' cemetery right next to it. But I saw far more evidence of peace in the new nation: women fighters serving in the government, children learning in their mother tongues, a grassroots constitution process coming to fruition, and so much more—developing itself with confidence, joy, and incredibly hard work. War *was* in Eritrea, but no more. At least for the next three years.

But on 5/6/98, as my poem so-titled observes, war returned, beginning as a border dispute between Eritrea and Ethiopia but expanding to consume at least 100,000 soldiers on both sides and displacing hundreds of thousands of people. Such horrific violence ended by mutual agreement in 2000, but a Hague-decreed "final and binding" verdict in 2002 that settled the border did not resolve hostilities.

The "Against All Odds" conference and its historic "Asmara Declaration on African Languages and Literatures" happened in 2000 despite the war, and I have been returning to Eritrea ever since despite a "no war—no peace" stalemate and an all but constant storm of international denunciation of the Eritrean government. Yet I have been returning because in Eritrea—where war was and even where war is—I have found that far more than war has sustained it through the years of European and African colonialism and for millennia—and still does, which the poems and translations in *Where War Was* reflect.

When I returned to Eritrea in September 2000, nine months after the "Against All Odds" conference yet three months into a shaky peace agreement, instead of brightness, buoyancy, and optimism filling the streets of Asmara as in 1995, I found deep anxiety and shocked disbelief that war had returned with such a vengeance. Six months after "Against All Odds," in May 2000, Ethiopia launched a massive military offensive resulting in the occupation not only of the disputed sections of the border between the two countries but also previously undisputed parts of Eritrea. Eritrea had survived worse, as one friend there reminded me, but other friends expressed their fears and disgust at the return to their country of war-displaced persons, bombed-out cities, deserted fields gone fallow, and, again, an enormous number of military casualties.

At this point, I might have changed my mind and/or taken back my words about Eritrea being a place "where war was," replacing them with "where war is," but it never dawned on me. What I saw in 1995 and recorded in the poem, "Where War Was," made me steadfast.

The outbreak of war in 1998 came at the height of the planning and development of the conference, "Against All Odds," and threatened to terminate the process. The war scared off many of the project's regional and international supporters, including governments, the UN, NGOs, foundations, corporations, universities, and more. After all, the massive Ethiopian attack in May 2000 could have happened five months before as the conference was taking place. In fact, one of its main events, "Orature in the Valley of the Sycamores: The Big Conversation," unfolded a mere ninety kilometers from where the Eritrean and Ethiopian armies lined up eye to eye and ready for war.

"Against All Odds," nevertheless, succeeded despite the palpable danger primarily because of the support of Eritrea itself. Eritreans had to mobilize, performing all the work that such a gathering required: students and faculty from the university, the unions of Eritrean youth and women, nearly every government ministry, local writers, musicians, dancers, businesses, clubs, state and city workers, and, as always, the *tegedelti*. Moreover, inside Eritrea, despite the conference's name, its actually happening was never "against all odds"—only outside Eritrea. Whatever the odds of this literature and language project, Eritreans, again, had dealt with worse, far worse. Thus, my experience of the unwavering support of Eritrea for the "Against All Odds" conference led me not to doubt in 2000 or ever thereafter that something more than war determined and defined the nation's character.

Not that there were not other reasons to have doubts. And I mean more serious challenges than the U.S. Department of State travel warnings against going to Eritrea that have been posted all the times I have journeyed there since 1998.

Planning to return to Eritrea in 2002 after the "Against All Odds" conference in 2000, I had two problems to confront: internal politics and the return of war in relation to Eritrean contemporary poetry.

First, Eritrean security forces had recently arrested a number of former and current government ministers. At the same time the government shut down all eight privately owned newspapers and detained their editors and reporters. Meanwhile, Zemhret Yohannes, the director of Eritrea's Research and Documentation Center and a good friend, invited me to come to Asmara to translate and edit an anthology of contemporary Eritrean poets. Should I accept his invitation? The most frequent answer I received in consulting with friends and colleagues, including those with whom I worked closely for years on "Against All Odds," without whose efforts it would not have developed and succeeded, was *no*. My literary work would be perceived to countenance when I should protest the arrests, the detentions, the imprisonments, the banning of a free press, and demonstrations and, furthermore, the postponement of elections and the ratification of the constitution. When I asked Reesom Haile if he thought I should pursue the project, he responded vehemently: "They'll use you as a symbol and parade you around as evidence that the country is still open and encouraging freedom of expression. They'll use you for propaganda." But I never thought of myself as that important. Would Eritrea, of all places and after all it had been through, use an outsider, a *ferenji* for cover after surviving a three-decade war with an Ethiopia backed at different times by both the Soviets and the Americans? Also, I had always tried, as much as possible, to be in the background with Africa in the foreground in my writing. Furthermore, I couldn't imagine how propaganda could make a good poem. If anything, it was a height of freedom of expression—linguistically, intellectually, and politically—and, of course, I would only want to include good poems in the anthology including Reesom's. He insisted that I would be pressured to exclude him although I never was.

Only one friend encouraged me to go to Eritrea in 2002 to continue my literary work: Larry Sykes, the very artist whose images grace *Where War Was*. It is the result of following his advice: "If you can . . . why not try? You have to go back. It's a part of the story you'll be missing all your life if you don't."

The second problem I thought I would have to confront in returning to Eritrea in 2002 was whether the subject of war, since it broke out again in 1998 and continued to roil everyday Eritrean life, would drive out everything else from the contemporary poetry. If this were the case, furthermore, the appeal of a new anthology of Eritrean war poetry could be limited, since the explicit, unless ironic or negative, depiction of war's violence had not been celebrated in poetry in English for nearly a century. No doubt privileging my own poetic orientation and preconceptions at the expense of the Eritrean experience, I still had to be realistic about whether the anthology would have international as well as national readers. Also, was the depiction of modern warfare as positive and celebratory, if not desirable, even possible in English anymore? For all of Reesom's popularity as a poet, both in the original Tigrinya and in English translations, while he wrote about the war's effects on his people, he did not write about war itself. Furthermore, some writers and readers in Eritrea considered this a shortcoming in his work. Zemhret, in fact, confirmed my suspicions that Eritrean war poetry would be a big part of a new anthology, but he also sensed the conflict between my desire to produce a representative anthology and my hesitation over the subject of war overwhelming the collection when he said, "These poets write a lot about the field and about war. And yet war isn't only about fighting. And it's not all about death. That's too restrictive. They write about friendship and the perennial issues of love and life. War has that, too."

"The perennial issues"—Eritrea has that, too. Could not the same observation be applied to many other places worldwide where the all too present warscape engenders the misconception that it is the sole perennial issue? The poems and translations of *Where War Was* reflect an Eritrea from the time I first experienced it, twenty years ago, through the renewed wartime around the millennium, to now, which is more than the all too prevalent representation of Eritrea as little if no more than a perennial warscape.

In war, at peace, or stuck in a situation of no war and no peace, Eritreans themselves provide a variety of answers for what has sustained their nation.

For the social scientist, Astier Almedom, it is one word: resilience. For the journalist, Said Abdelhay, it is "our voice . . . heard through more than a gun." For the attorney and law professor, Senai Ademariam, it is biblical, in a famous passage from *Leviticus* 6:13—"The fire shall ever be burning upon the altar; it shall never go out." For the women's activist and government official, Senait Lijam, it is "armed struggle," which she characterizes as not only armed struggle with a gun but also "with a pen. You can be armed with an idea. You can be armed with a notion of social justice. You can be armed with commitment. You can be armed with steadfastness."

For Eritrea's greatest historian, Alemseged Tesfai, it is "the heart" of an Eritrean soldier that he found in 1988 during the battle

> *of Afabet, under an indistinguishable shrub . . . a piece of flesh amid a pool of dried and curdled blood. . . . complete with aorta and arteries: one that had poured out what blood it had been pumping into the veins of a fighter who had been blown to pieces by falling artillery fire. . . . Disturbing to look at or talk about even today . . . that ugly product and specimen of unwanted and unnecessary violence. . . . [T]he heart lying there triumphant and heroic, but strangely in that hour of total victory and glory, also lonely, lonely and defiant.*

Alemseged's "heart" of Eritrea is fundamental to its people, languages, history, nationalism, and his own writing.

> *[T]he heart is not just a life-giving organ. In Tigrinya, a wise man or wise woman is called* lebam, *and wisdom is* lebona. *They both come from the word* lebi, *which means heart. In Tigre,* laleb *is the word for a wise person. It comes from* leb, *which means the heart. In Billen, a wise person is called* labekukh, *which comes from* labahkah, *which means the heart. Like all humanity we think with our heads, but we say we think with our hearts. The heart is the creator. The pen is the creation of the heart. When I speak of the pen, I speak of the heart. I speak of how the Eritrean heart acted throughout the struggle. Performance also is the performance of the heart. Eritrean history is a struggle between forces that have been trying to write off Eritrea as a nation, to simply ignore it as something that did not exist, and the heart of Eritreans that refused to bend to these forces of destruction. As a writer I will speak from the heart.*

An Eritrea of "perennial issues of love and life" where war was or where war is can also be heard in the poem, actually a transcription of a performance in 2000 by Zeineb Yassin, a veteran fighter and mother of nine, at "Against All Odds" in 2000 when she was 82. To a crowd of thousands gathered under a massive sycamore tree, she describes herself but inevitably her nation as "too bold in this damn world."

For Reesom Haile, his nation of Eritrea is best known through "Our Language":

> *The sauce*
> *With spicy melted*
> *Butter,*
> *Berbere pepper*
> *And sea salt.*
> *The bones are big*
> *Not only for the flavor.*
> *But take them*
> *Like communion.*

So I continue to say, "Join here and write."

POEMS

WHERE WAR WAS

1. What Remained

"Daddy, up . . . bird . . . nest . . . worm"—without a war?
My children laugh to birdsong in the sunshine.
Can we start all over without a war?
Easy as a morning visit to the tailor,
Bronze and creamy in his silk vest and jacket,
Measuring our whole family for new outfits?
A long and easy meal on a mild afternoon,
Outside on the water, wine whenever we want,
The wilds in our voices and other myths of love
Blending into the moment, without a war?
A nap in the shade on sacks bursting with grain,
As finches and sparrows fly in for a feed;
Grapes spilling over the walls onto a street,
And a girl laughing at her face in a mirror?
Without a war? Nothing to do but sit
And play in the tidal pools without a war?
Our land and needs thriving on each other
Without a missile? The minerals, fuel, silver,
And gold—with understanding seeping like earth
And tasting like us on our lips without a war?
Without a war, night and day, working or dancing?

I would laugh like a child if this could be an art:
If it could start, stop, and never be a weapon,
Greased by no fear, no wisdom, and no knowing
That once upon a time there was a murder—
Us—with sand drifting over and a storm to flee—
Us—chewing rags, eyes cried out of their sockets—
Ours—right limbs yanking out left limbs, bones
Breaking each other—us—murderers and murdered—
Us and ours—separating as we separated;
The scar tearing its way down the forehead
Through the eyebrow and deep into the half face
That a rifle butt blinded and left behind:
Surrounded near and far by the mechanical

Reproduction of soldier after soldier and their armory
Stenciled with every supernationality
In the graveyard waiting to burst open
At the return of the one and only power;
Or some one and only power, if it appears. . . .

Clinging to our prickly pear escarpment, we saw
War and peace like two sides of the same picture:
The impulse to survive the next moment
Of kill or be killed, conquered or craving,
Regardless of the conflagration and ashes
Necessary for an unimaginable victory
Against destruction nevertheless certain
If we didn't make ourselves empty as deserts,
Anything but imagined, and even more certain,
Seeing the best and cheapest form of execution:
Forbidding anyone to touch the streams
So our crops fail year after year after year;
And purging the factory workers of their souls:
Scrambling their father and son religions
With concessions and pounding them home
With the threat of heavy artillery to replace
A simple dream of getting the family cow
Off a muddy road onto a raft in a river.

Half a breath and one step more would lead
To our large hometown that rarely saw a robbery
And never murder twisted into an all public and politicized
Temple of state terror where people counted
As nothing, with or without a nation or
Even its illusion . . . unless it reminded them—
Whether their place existed now or not—
Of enduring, when they knew they couldn't, to begin
A new economy of prosthetics for no limbs
And pads for the everyday blood without a war:
Whatever the dry shrunken pear once a brain
Still rattling in the skull, yet now without a war,
As lightning joined the arc and triangle,
And all but inaudible—except when laughing—

The combat voice not supposed to be for combat
Needed neither to fight nor to prove itself
To be equal, win or lose, fighting or not.

Child of a nation or nation of a child, no one
Could prepare enough for such horror and healing,
Forgetting and not forgetting the perished,
Following or not the tracks of a nomad
With a sick child on a homemade stretcher—
From nowhere to nowhere, a lifetime's savings
Of fake gold riveted through all too many veils
From all directions, above and below, inside and out?
In total isolation allowed to own
Nothing, go hungry, rarely to sleep, choose
Nothing, never breathe free, go nowhere alone
Without being mutilated, blood poisoned,
And forbidden the market? Every delicate curve
Peeled like an egg, eaten, and thrown away like the shell?
Shy and dying young, denied experience's
Simple stool, little room, and every lesson in a book?
Endurance? Resilience? Something more
Than being an inevitable victim: more than destroyed
Or abandoned from the beginning—enough to let
The cross sights rust and spider webs steer a way
To the cannon tires rotting without a war where war was?

2. *We Embrace*

Where war was we embrace in the dry riverbeds,
Our tents pitched colorless amidst the bougainvillea—
Salmon, fuchsia, tangerine, yellow, pink, and white—
And combing out some peace in the mimosa:
Near the cypress of no grief, promising measure
And wine again—where war, leaving our tools worthless
And our animals without grain, stopped all the milk
For anthrax and miscarriage to rule
The groves of papaya and oranges with bamboo
Patches where we fought the lonely tanks exploding
At each other in the waves of bleaching heat.

Half kisses and half flies filled the canyons owned
By no one except war and the same old diseases
Daubing blood on the waist-high, half boulder huts
Camouflaged by plastic, paper, and grass
Near the vegetable fields camouflaged in land mines.
Where war was we embrace in the dry riverbeds
With eyes like trees more gnarled than their roots
And with our terrible poverty invisible
But gaping like an empty umbrella frame
Of thorn trees with a broken branch to stir
A pot of battery patina to paint our portraits
In their shade, shared like a still life, *nature morte*,
Of a gun barrel and a donkey carcass thin as a glove.

Where war was we embrace in the dry riverbeds
And love like the roads on fire and packed everyday
With clouds of goats descended from brown skies,
Treeless mountains, and people speaking the unspeakable
But only in the shade of a rock where war was.
It twitched them eaten alive by hunger
And made the dry riverbeds where we embrace
Watched by lizards guarding half wrecked bridges
Into a theatre of skeleton games and parades
With thousands dropping dead along the way—
Corpses everywhere in ragged sacks and smothered
In crows until we came with gasoline
To burn what there was too much of to bury.
We walked away, ripped by the thorns, our bodies
Blackened in the blaze. . . . But it died, too, and today
We embrace in the dry riverbed and play
Like water: water dug deep in time with our hands—
Resurrecting water where war was, where war was. . . .
More and more water dug by many hands to flow
To a city to unite what before could exist no more.

With war spontaneously made *was* and dreams of peace
Made flesh all at once we jump up and down—
Dancing to dance like leaves, leaves of flags
And flags of leaves dreamed out of our mouths

Between kisses, daughters and sons now safe
On the streets at all hours. Look, the president
Can walk alone in sandals amidst our buildings
Like pianos, their creamy shine trimmed green and gold
And our mirrors trimmed with frost. Look, each face
Brilliantly strikes its own different angle.
See us leaning on the turquoise formica counters
For strong coffee, city beer, saxophones, and
Each other remaking the music of our night
Free of the constant fire of automatic weapons
And worse: the funeral cortege day after day—
No sound but muffled drums, hoof clatter, rumbling
Iron wheels, and bells tolling bells tolling bells
Until they echo like a last resort of self-reliance.

Where war was, the swallows and blowing chartreuse buds
Scatter new ways into life for the bombed-out buildings
In restoration to the roar of loaded buses and trucks.
The eyes of bullet-holed walls see peace on the move again.
The pastel metal doors of packed and noisy schools
Swing open with no need to defy and plenty of bread—
With no fear in the expectation of a mistake
That won't let us ever see our home and rest
On the front steps again—not hurt but safe,
Free of the blame or desire in fundamental belief
Where war was but is no longer the only thing:
The only word—like a cryptogram of terror
And inhumanity spelled in every ideology.

3. *Their Echoes*

Let every source of any word open within
Walking distance, unthreatened by the crazy
Or homeless, who walk there, too, and unpunished
By taking away our books, paper, pencils, and computers
For a swamp to break back through the surface
We thought had been written every day in marble.
Let no rhetoric of obligation and niceties
Based on hate keep us from our golden domes

And mosaicked rocks, our oldest olive trees—
The fig and pomegranate shade free of guilt
And the walls that hold our beloved dead.
Yet where war was, memory and forgetting
Glow like a door and window in a universal
Hovel: a home denied, unknown, unrecognized,
Not worth anyone's breath or talking about,
Yet where war was and where we were with no lies:
No lies for cripples—all of us cripples, defectives
Life-sentenced to piss alleys, building trash,
Burst columns, cast off stones, industrial pus,
Breathing exhaust, depths of shit, asbestos wrap,
Mercury, linoleum, slaughterhouses, salty pollution,
Rusted away screens, walls of smoke, taped pots
Full of ash, the only light down the floor drains,
And everything denied but the last breath of hunger
Lingering over the steaming vats of sour milk
Fenced off behind the absent landlord's dairy.
Tin cans on a string crisscross the sidewalk outside
And rattle for armed guards to rush into the street,
Led by their dog of a leader dressed in apples and bananas.
The town overlooks the graveyard it must become,
Already stacked with ammunition crates of human bones
Mostly skulls and legs, some still wearing boots.

Where war was leads to a city of women
Decimated of their men, strangled by piano wire,
Cigarette burns on the hands and necks of our little boys,
Most minds gone, girls gang raped and found in the morning
With their breasts cut off, left in the street near their homes—
Their eyes missing, stabbed or shot in a panicky last minute.
Where war was, the only human right as if it were divine,
Is torture, rabid murder, teeth ripping human flesh,
A dangling windpipe, a docile butcher to process
Suspenders out of skin and buttons of children's bones.
In the gravel of a dry day on a dry afternoon
How about a hose stuffed down the throat?
Why not kill a baby that will die of thirst
And any other animal needing to be taken care of?

Destroy the ovens, smash all the dishes and jugs.
Spill out all the grain. It's a stash for grenades.
Choose which children to feed or let die.
Where war was leads us to the execution
Unhesitating, unsuspecting, unquestioning.
It's always the same except in trivial details:
A given; the jerked out pistol point blank
To the head; the firing squad anxious to be ordered
And told to aim only at the diamond encrusted heart
To avoid excessive blood; the blasts again and again—
Reloading and blinded in the wild smoke.
Is anyone left not deaf and powder burned?
Run up to the bodies; more shots to the heads,
Pounding rifle butts, stick in the bayonets.
Make a mash of skull, hair, brain, and blood.
Strip the bodies, wrap them in sheets, gag or not,
And throw them with sulfuric acid in a brick-lined pit.
Watery warm mud and the summer heat
Bloat the remains impossibly big, except for their sex,
With flies, maggots, and eggs where there used to be a face.
What's next? Again the story is all repeats.
Do we dig up their bones? Are they saints? Mistakes?
To divide? Unite? Are we this churned mud?
In the middle of a road among dark pools?
Without a war? Where war was? Without a war?

Where war was? Without a war, a debate
Ensues excluding no one, and an old man
Sits with his one useful leg and a walking stick.
His eyes the color of dawn, his body at dusk,
And his old clothes draping him like peace,
He looks out from a corner of his yard
On nearby goats and terracing red earth,
Fully aware of the mercy allowing him a pulse.
He welcomes and pities whomever he meets,
Saying, "Without a war. Use what's left.
Tons of scrap metal, crazy angled masonry.
Cut hair. Wastebaskets. Shredded plastic. Bricks.
A baby boy's or baby girl's first breath."

Without a war, where war was, he shuffles up the steps
When asked to show the new school he built. He frescoed
The front with four maps—his town, nation, continent, and the world:
All the same size, only in different scales.
He also shows the hospital he built where there was none.
Like a little motel of different adjoining rooms
For a pharmacy, storage, labor, delivery, pre-op,
Operating, inoculations, recovery, rest,
And everyone in them dead without them—though he adds,
"Still only some of the poor and solving only one of their problems."
Outside and up the rocky paths, children play
Without a war or anyone needed to watch them.
Their shouting comes through the dust, "All right.
All right. All right. All right. All right."
The mountains wrap themselves around their echoes.

5/6/98

Back to war.
Shut the door.

Forgive, forget before?
Now remember twice—

Then and now.
Shut the door.

Children free?
No more.

Forget before.
Now remember twice—

Spikes in the brain,
Locks on the knots,

Trees in full bloom
Break at the waist.

"Nation" translates
Into "hatred."

Dark bursts of rain,
No gold and silver waves of grain—

Back to war.
Shut the door.

HALF THE LINKS

Half the links
Of my father's watch chain
Flew into the tree.

Can I think
Away the watch and his pain
And dream him happy?

At the brink
I break a branch in vain.
My mother watches me.

Please, no winks.
I'm leaving again
For a new country.

ADULITE

1. *Tree*

Ancient gripped in granite
To perform pure mass,
Vast sycamore in the fields
Where spots with no grass
Mean walls lie underneath,
And where I have kneeled,
I tell you my loves and fears
Because the names come from here.

2. *Well*

Dear ancient well
That garbage fills,
Mere hole in the ground,
Great document
Read from the top
But reread from the deep,
I follow the way you held
Water, now gone but spelled
In the sand leading back
To life still the same
At the Safra dam:
Girl, boy, water,
Jug, dip, carry,
Word, and stone;
The "I am"
Without the fire.

3. *gTmi / Joining / Poetry*

Granite and sycamore join
Up the trunk and down to the loins.

Children laugh and climb
The hard and the soft seams

Like *verba* and *res*—
They rhyme.

From limb to limb,
Blossoms, fruit,
Green leaves, and dry
Continually
Go round the tree.

The oldest example
Of our language
Inscribes a stele
In a field below:
strug l agains al od s wi

Stands out
With the sun
And a quarter moon—
Adulite.
Join here and write.

POE IN MASSAWA

In state his glory well befitting,
The ruler of the realm was seen.
            Edgar Allan Poe, "The Haunted Palace"

Square with seven arches on each side
Of marble and blue enamel,
The emperor's palace says he died
Horribly but lived well.
The grand entrance stairs blasted in two,
The gaping dome, bullet holed, crumbling
Walls, and missing floors the light pours through
Recall a King of Kings

Who rarely slept, fed conspirators
To his leopards and lions at dawn,
Acted peacefully amidst total war,
Scattered flamingoes across his lawns,
Lived without the written word,
Barely spoke, and punished silence.
He only remembered
What he thought made sense

And strengthened him as head of state.
Anything else meant disease.
He also thought it wisdom to wait,
Seeing everyone on their knees
Had a knife behind their back.
But now the railings' shattered filigree,
A foundation full of cracks,
And viscera of masonry

Dangling in oriental doors
Speak of a greater power here.
It says, ignore.
Climbing on a balcony, I peer
Through the shutters at a rich table
And chairs lined up, but nobody comes.

The elevator without car and cables
And the belfry stripped deaf and dumb

Faze no one, and a shirtless man
Walks by barefoot in a sarong.
A delivery van
And a boat in dry dock don't seem to belong
Next to the palace, but they portend
No more spirit
To haunt him and the fishing dhows that bend
Among the container ships that sit

In the harbor doing business
Or haunting you and me
As we join a chorus
Of camels silhouetted against the sea,
Particles clinging to a grinding stone . . .
And a raven's nevermore
In a corner of the emperor's bones
Upon the Red Sea shore.

SEEING THINGS

The missing panes
On an abandoned greenhouse
Still reflect the dusk.

No one in the youth orchestra
Misses a note
When the lights go out.

Ready to go,
An old man holds a closed atlas
On a Monday morning.

Traffic pounds the bridge,
And round stones
Line the river below.

Painted on the coffin's inside,
The sun from between her legs
Departs through her arms.

SbuQ nr'esu kfu'e nr'esu.
Your good comes back to you,
And your bad does, too.

FOGNATURA

Traveling, passing the portals
Of dissociation and older
Than anyone I see, alone
And in a language not my own,
Why end up here again? Abstract
Except for the pangs of leaving
Home? The reasons have no effect.
The eloquence of the unknown
Takes over. Call it *fognatura*.

First come dancers and fires hissing
At each other in the morning.
Pulled one way and bowed another,
Horsehair strings on a hollow gourd
Lure the last surviving player
Of the soft wood horn with a brass,
Battered, and old mouthpiece to blast
The sky six times, and then it pours.
Rivers form along the roads.
They flood, deeper and deeper.

"Were there no sewers?" I keep thinking.
Then I see the rivers turn gold.
The swallows and buildings turn gold.
The water and the air—all gold. . . .

The gutters finally drain, but
Later, my vision remaining
Like a new skeleton to keep
An old skeleton company,
I see a manhole: the steel lid
Embossed with FOGNATURA.
Is it the manufacturer?
Back then I am not sure: *fognatura*—
The word for sewer and also a slur.

MASSAWA

Senbet'se bahri ikwa te'ref (On Sunday even the sea rests)

Sundays in July, nothing moves
In Massawa, even the sea.
Allowing no color, dawn pulls down
The coral villas' bamboo shades.
Forget any screens or windows.
Black-headed storks, enemy planes,
And ravens glue themselves solid
To a sky like brittle paper.
No news, no info, no issue—
So what if food aid
Rots on the docks, battleships
Come to call, medics can't help
Mothers getting dehydrated,
The government really is
Nothing but rebels, suicide
Bombers recruit at the bus stops,
And the amputees get less and less?
Sundays in July, nothing moves.
The name "port" no longer applies.
Who needs security?
Two women shuffling down the street?
Or two men swimming off the heat?
A boy chasing a soccer ball
Through the debris of three arches?
The emperor's palace no one uses?
The Red Sea salt for sale?
The one person wearing shoes
Instead of sandals?
An unidentifiable car
Ploughed into a palm tree,
Dead or alive who can tell?
Still life rules the day,
And even the memories
Of massacred children and liberation
Equally fade away

Like ideas instead of things.
Nothing moves.
Differences don't register:
Air and sea temperature—the same;
Long phrases droning from the mosques,
The ringing bells of four St. Mary's;
Stray cats and wandering camels;
Tourists on the beaches and a girl
Chasing a chicken past huts of
Sticks, plastic, and rust.
Two crouching men and a donkey
Join the ruling party drinking from
The same well with no change to come.
Businesses, bulletins, machines,
Schedules, marching, and longing
Have no place here: no one to show
What they mean and no one to feel
Anything except being unreal.
Sundays in July, nothing moves
In Massawa, even the sea,
And I weep at so much peace.

RETURN TO ROME

I.

Petrarch would never have wanted only Latin to say this:
Barbara pyramidum sileat miracula Memphis.
Petrarch would use his Italian to say, "Barbaric Memphis,
Praise of the pyramids as if they were miracles should stop."

I saw a monument in Arezzo, built in the twenties
By Mussolini to Petrarch as if he wrote in Latin:
Rome's nursing she wolf beside him, standard Mother and Child,
Medieval knights and heroic nudes inscribed with the paunchy
Dictator's fantasy: *"Roma caput mundi"*—a nightmare.
But something else carved near Petrarch sounded much more creative.
I read the words *"Nostro Capo Roma"* out loud to myself,
Honoring Petrarch as first to write his poetry the way
Poets in Europe and any since must follow: in their own
Language like Petrarch's Italian and not anyone else's,
Faking what should come directly from the sense of their own tongue.

II.

Petrarch would never have wanted only Latin to say this:
Africa semper aliquid novi—but in Italian
He might say, translated into English: "Something new always
Comes out of Africa," and he might have said it of my friend
From Eritrea in Rome for doctors there to save his life.

Thirty-year veteran of fighting Ethiopia, my friend
Struggled for freedom and triumphed, standing by his small nation
Fighting the US and Russians, too, their proxy wars feeding
Geopolitical fires still burning, with Eritrea
Still forced to fight for its life, depending only on itself
And no one else in a world that barely knows Eritrea,
Where it appears on the map or who might live there like my friend:
Battlefield graduate of the only university
Found to be credible—revolution; marrying there, too,
Raising a son with his fighter wife and dealing with the day

Bombs hit their valley and shrapnel nearly blinded him for life.
Two decades later my friend served as a Marxist Medici,
Helping the writers and artists of Asmara to survive.

I hadn't visited Rome for twenty years, but I had come
When I was younger and searching for a spiritual home.
Ten times at least I had stayed there, hoping never to depart.
But if I now had a place away from home and my children,
Barbara, Bethlehem, and whatever else I had become,
Might I say Africa? Eritrea? Now where I traveled
Even more frequently since my last trip long ago to Rome?
Why was I calling Asmara, "Rome's Rome?" What was I feeling?
"Africa's Africa" back in my old spiritual home?

Thirty-five years ago with my parents, on my first visit,
Speeding through Traforo tunnel, I looked out of the back seat
Into the darkness, but what if I could see myself walking
Now on the sidewalk and holding hands with Barbara amidst
Bellowing traffic that sounded like Fellini's in *Roma*?
I was obsessed with religious art, so would I have even
Recognized I was myself, and nearly my father's age then?
What would I think of four children, our belonging to no church,
What we were wearing to dinner, what we thought of the Forum—
Seeing an arrogant nation like our own come to ruin
(Hopelessly commonplace feeling, therefore, seeming all too true)
And the idea of an endless chain of history in things
Equally there to exalt, my favorite being the frescoes
Up on the fourth floor of Rome's *Palazzo Massimo alle
Terme*, and Barbara's being little churches with paintings
Filling the ceilings, and maybe work by Caravaggio
Off in a corner and waiting to be patiently worshipped?

Now that I came back to Rome, I walked through set after set of
Dreams less forgotten and more real than the past I remembered.

One afternoon when we met my friend and after espressos,
Several times as we walked and let him choose the way to go,
We would be stopped at a corner or enjoying some baroque
Detail we never before had noticed—typical of Rome—

When he would say to me, "*La citta eterna*," with a smile.
"*Roma*," I answered him, "*La citta eterna*," and later
Three times at dinner we toasted, "To the *citta eterna*."
As we were walking, I felt like we were walking forever:
As if the afterlife—"The eternal city"—could be true:
As if it started already here and now and continued
Simply with walking together in *la citta eterna*.
It didn't matter he lost a lot of weight, and he shuffled,
His pants too baggy as if he could be merely another
African immigrant hustling me, a tourist, around Rome.

III.

Petrarch would never have wanted only Latin to say this:
Carthago delenda est, or "Carthage has to be destroyed."
Petrarch would use his Italian to embellish such a curse,
As I imagined it booming in the air of a painting
By the Italian Michele Cammarano, whom we found
Coincidentally next day after seeing my good friend.

Following him to *Piazza Cinquecento,* half circling
Termini Station, and thinking "*Cinquecento*" referred to
Art or more simply the 1500s, I heard the story
How in Dogali the Eritreans, thousands and well-armed,
Slaughtered five hundred Italian soldiers, put there to quickly
Conquer the country in 1887 with no one
Able to stop them, which Cammarano's painting depicted.
Shocked by the massacre and in mourning, Italy tried to
Honor the casualties with a granite, middling obelisk,
As my friend showed us, where we could see the *memento mori*
Set on a pedestal glass and garbage strewn, though it couldn't
Dampen our wanting to see it closer and the inscriptions:
All of the names in Italian, *cinquecento*, dead in Dogali.
Then I remembered when I was there, and in Eritrea
That little hilltop and monument seemed much less important—
With its inscriptions, Tigrinya and Italian side by side—
Than the few camels and two historic bridges in the dust.
In the same spirit of "*Roma caput mundi*" on Petrarch's
Monument, and in the 1920s, too, Mussolini

Ordered the obelisk moved from right in front of the station
To a small park on the side. *Eroi* failing to survive
Africa, meeting the eyes of Romans, wasn't a vision
Fascism wanted to face, yet neither did Cammarano's
Painting, which took up a whole wall of the *Arte Moderna*'s
Room twenty-three in the "Giordano Bruno" *salone*.
Finishing in 1895, supposedly after
Five years of living in Eritrea, did Cammarano
Paint what he saw near Massawa, or what Italy had dreamed
Africa always would look like from *la citta eterna*?
White gloves and uniforms, sashes, scarves, and earnest Italians
Mustached and falling down hills too green and under a blue sky?
Falling in foregrounds where coal black Eritreans blend into
Still blacker horses: an apelike mass with leopard skins and tails;
Brute force with scimitars, spears, and Colonel De Cristoforis
Plunging his sword as if he alone could never be destroyed?

THE FUNERAL OF ISAYAS TSEGAI

I'm not important. My time to talk ends now: in Asmara,
Cinema Odeon, no one at the marble and mirrored
Bar, the espresso machine not working, dim, and two dozen
Stainless steel, gold-flecked formica tables empty except for
Three or four students, Italian movie posters with cleavage
Deep in ripped blouses, and early 90s action film heroes,
Mostly American peeling from the *trompe l'oeil* and cracked walls.
Irony and the sincere at peace can share this lobby, too.
"Literature, Power, Translation, Eritrea" is my theme,
I mean my lecture, the reason why I come here this July
Morning, enjoying the cool air—but where is everybody?
Going outside again, I approach Berhane, my friend, and
Ask, but he whispers, "Isayas Tsegai died without warning
Last night, and everyone wants to be at his house this morning.
Come to his funeral noon tomorrow—Patriot's Cemetery."

Translating lines of his poems, "I Am Also a Person"
And "Lamentation," ten years ago; and meeting him later:
Anything but that forsaken voice of war in his *Limon
Limony*, first book of poems—grisly soldier on the cover,
Mountains and deserts around him, crouched and watering a tree;
Giving the book to me, and my giving it to the library,
Which couldn't read the Tigrinya Ge'ez script of the title—
Meaning it couldn't be catalogued until I translated.

Anything but: and I don't mean epic films and TV shows,
Cinematography, music, theater, his revolution's
Painful and most private moments loading rifts of his vision
From the screen all the way back to "I Am Also a Person."
When I read its first translation, words burst senselessly except
For their emotion, which I believed, but English words had lost
During the World Wars—and so I tried to locate them again
In my translation—for better, worse? That's not for me to say.
Neither is elegy on Isayas—that's for the joiners,
Poets of *Ertra*: their *melkes*, not mine. Anything but. Please!

Not the Isayas Tsegai of life—his funeral moves these

Minor heroics: in this case going back where I started
When I first came to Asmara. Lectures, witnessing, writing
Fifteen years on the centrality of literature lasting
Thousands and thousands of years in Eritrea, and seeing
Western eyes usually dart away or glaze as a result—
Planning to further these themes that fateful morning had to stop.
Back to my being like what I came here for in the first place:
Listening—tasting and seeing, but not talking; the only
Role that a non-native speaker should want in the beginning,
And which returns at the most important moments thereafter,
Like when this lecture goes unattended. Otherwise, who needs
Misuse and misinformation? Working not inside-out but
Stuck and cursed always at outside-in and mattering nothing,
Whether important or not, except for loss, waste, and no love,
Nursing a heart twisted like a road through mountainous desert?

Claiming authority based on reading, only misreading
For ideology—no exceptions/no surprise endings—
Doomed to whatever *reductio ad absurdam* it pleases.
Warranting *non grata* black or white depending on the day?
Seeking destabilization of whatever's not itself?
Showing off prowess, tradition, all as its own exceptions,
Not merely thwarted illusions worn as old scary masks?
Murder the renaissance rather than embracing its spirit—
Innocence and the original recovered at long last?

How about this for a manifesto? Will and a conscience sing
On the horizon. Precision and conviction unravel
What we divine and think deep in hibernation while sketching
Words in the ashes: Isayas' "I am also a person."
Then being quiet to join the ranks that form for his funeral.
Armies and empires like Red Sea foam and clouds in the highlands—
Water in Sahel (again, that cover's soldier pours water)
Lasting the same, and I'm dreaming something else could be for me?

Yes, and who doesn't, which leads to seeing this funeral's greatness.
Not that it needs any recognition offered by me, but
Also vice versa is true—an honest, lonely equation—
Knowing millennialist strife and bloodshed plaguing this country,

Likewise the present and ancient letters, voices, and stories,
Mostly invisible like the archeology thus far,
Must be impervious, no more yielding than the surroundings—
Not the romantic, pathetic answers aching hearts require.
Still there's the funeral: something more than death is life, bread not
Poems, the eloquent voices cut off one by one, claiming
Some other meaning than guns against each other's oblivion. . . .

Late at night, died in his office, writing, never recovered
Consciousness: stroke—and by dawn, I still had not gotten the word?
(See what I mean about crossing the sincere and ironic?)

Thousands and thousands of men and women thirty-six hours
Later have gathered to form a long procession from the church—
Orthodox under the Eritrean flag—as they follow
Body and flowers in two black minivans through the stucco
Walls of the graveyard: the men in western clothes and the women
Wrapped in traditional white and gauzy dresses with ribbons
Hemming their similar shawls. The men and women stay separate,
Never together until they reach the grave, where I'm hoping
Not to be visible. But instead my friends say I should be,
Pushing me into the front row, nodding, "Look. You should see it."
Was that the message, the din of weeping, wailing, the crackling
Eulogies straining the metal speakers strung up on high poles;
Bricks lining six open graves, a growing mountain of flowers
Next to Isayas'; his rest in peace or chaos all the same,
Like the wind, red clay, and sunshine—indistinguishably hard,
Too bright and cold while the children who had joined the Isayas'
Theater group break through the crowd to throw themselves in his
    grave—
All while the orthodox priests in day-glo shimmering vestments,
Waving their censers and loudly chanting barely could be heard?

After the funeral, mourners filled the restaurants, cafés,
And all the bars in Asmara. Join them can be the only option.

Later out on a savannah I hear *anima mea*
Dominum . . . "my soul, the Lord" and then *magnificat*, meaning
"Magnify." Meaning? The vast and arid flatness like a scroll

Mottled with shrubs and all spindly tressed, unrolling the plateaus'
Green and blue sluiced by dark valleys into more plateaus and farmed
Mattock by mattock and hand by hand or maybe if lucky
Some wooden plough and a longhorn cow devoted to the lash?
Meaning the poverty in between "who am I" and fingers
Inch by inch tending their tiny plots beside their one-room homes?
Meaning a lifetime? A living based on pennies from selling
Baskets of prickly pears, peanuts in a bottle cap, gum, and
Throw in a stray pack of matches? What is all this resilience?
All this resilience—the healthcare, satellite TV, new schools,
Women's rights, positive change, and more help on its way—or not?
Lecturer in my off-white suit, t-shirt, colorful sneakers,
With my computer and iPod, iPad, iPhone in my bag,
I know I'm helpless to cross this great impassable divide.
Forward or backward or nothing moving? What am I seeing?
How can this scene be so glowing? Is it only last night's rain?
What am I hearing? That theme? Does it belong so strangely here?
Like a fantasia? What's that language? Is it my own, pure,
Under the spell of another, yet expanded and deepened?
It's so remote, but remaking it this way why do I feel free?

TRANSLATIONS OF POEMS

Zeineb Yassin
UNDER THE SYCAMORES

I'm burning
To boil you

Like raw,
Delicate meat
In liberation.

But I'm too old
For the army,

Too helpless
To be the secretary
Of education,

And too bold
In this damn world.

Saba Kidane
WAR AND A WOMAN

Of war and a woman I sing—
Only a woman
Can bring
Peace to my country.

Only a woman
Can sacrifice enough
To overcome fear,
Win the fight,
And still keep peace in sight.

Ready for anything,
She sacrifices herself
And gives birth,
Rocking and soothing
Like a lion

Licking her cubs,
Who grow with her love.
But peace
Demands more,
Calling her back

To the trenches.
Guarding her children,
She still can't refuse
To fight
Or even think

Of being tired,
Parched, starved,
Hurt, or dead.
Instead
She takes a breath

And catches fire,
Her breasts bouncing
As she runs
To join the fighters
Marching again—

Marching with her,
Marching for peace.

Reesom Haile
ANGEL FIQRIEL

Abducting brides? *Passe.*
These days you should pray,

"Angel of love,
With your bow and arrow,
Do you see what I see?
Please bring my love to me.

Empty your quiver.
Aim right for the heart
And open the bud.
Look! It bleeds,
Blooms, and bursts into seed."

Love works this way,
Although the priest doesn't know,
Hung up on Satan and the angels
Michael and Gabriel.

But if the priest asks, tell him
Your modern love poem.
If he asks about the part
With the angel who likes to pierce,
Ask the priest,

"Is my angel, Fiqriel, as fierce
As Michael, who cuts off heads?"

Reesom Haile
TELL THE PRESIDENT

In America they say,
Dream and make
Your dreams come true.
They call it
The American Dream.

In Africa they say,
The President dreams
Everything for you
And calls it
The African Dream.

Cream of Africa,
Who dream
Of going to America,

Tell the President.
Shoot your own gun!
My son, my daughter,
Go west with the sun.

Reesom Haile
HER PICTURE

I wrote to Photo Studio
In The Hague,

Dear Photographer:

Make a portrait
Of my Eritrea—
An African,

But she won't blacken your lens.
Fresh skin,
Full blooded and brown,

She glistens.
Her teeth and wide eyes
Gleam.

I want her head to toe,
The whole body,
Not one of your Mona Lisas.

Forget the Venus de Milo.
Reveal the beauty
Of her hands

And her figure
As she stands,
Crushes a snake
With her heel
Like Mother Mary,
And looks at me.

Also show how colors flash
From her dress
With her shawl, kerchief, and sash.

Patience, Photo Lucas
And Foto Zula
In Asmara.
She's in Europe now,

But some day
Ambling down Liberation Avenue,
She'll come to you
For her picture.

Reesom Haile
ONE

One, I say:
One by one, one plus,
One times, one minus,
One divided by. . . .
One.
I know arithmetic.

But I also I know history:
One.
We are *One,*
The Amharic king said,
As he invaded Eritrea.
Thus began our struggle
For independence.

I hear it said again:
One—
The reason
For gathering my people
Like wood for the fire.

I have learned:
One is no good
Without *freedom.*

Reesom Haile
JESUS' LAST WORDS

"My God, my God,
Why hast thou forsaken me?"
You said it, Jesus.
Now I see what you mean.

How's this for bread?
Taste this cup.
Talk about pain?

Your court was crooked,
But at least you got a trial.
My heroes rot in jail,
Or tomorrow they're locked up—

Nobody knows where,
And the court doesn't care.
It sets no trial date.

"My God, my God,
Why hast thou forsaken me?"
You said it, Jesus.
Now I see what you mean.

Reesom Haile
AFRICAN ANTHEM

Rainbow, rainbow
Where have you been?
My mother needs a sash
To match her skin.

A shower of colors
To catch her eye,
A garment of light,
Across the sky—

Shining like her face,
Streaming from the sun,
Seven different colors,
To reflect my special one.

One color's not enough—
Nor one without the other.
All of them must be
Worthy of my mother.

Rainbow, rainbow
Where have you been?
My mother needs a sash
To match her skin.

Reesom Haile
ERITREA'S DAUGHTER

Peace
Eritrea's daughter
Says what is
God her witness

Peace
She knows the worst
Goes hungry
Feeds her children first

Peace
Eritrea's daughter
Makes a home
For young and old

Peace
Eritrea's daughter
Drips her honey
Greater than Eritrea's gold

Eritrea's daughter
Also knows war
Forgets fear
Wears a bandoleer

Peace
Eritrea's daughter
Love her in all you do
And she drips honey on you

Reesom Haile
POVERTY

I have nothing.
Taste it with me.
If we share, we can bear
The worst poverty.

Why run away
And not even say
"God Bless. Good day?"
Why choose
Greed over me?

Weldedingel
WHAT CAN I CALL YOU?

What can I call you?
Why even say your name
Since you've died?

Can it be *Mount Sayim*?
Like a strong, angry woman
Elbowing out of the way
And ready to plow under
Any man who comes close.

Or should I call you *Mount Matara*?
Ready to yoke us in iron
If we don't scream and run.

Can I call you *Mount Keshi'at*?
Your hungry hands
Twist our spines
And twirl our necks
Like soft dough.

Or why not call you *Mount Zeri-Mosi*?
Showing no mercy
Like the devil in a deep lake
And the high-flying eagle.

Can I call you *Mount Bet Shama'ti*?
The sweet voice
Of a lovable spirit
Tempting his prey
Into a cave
And exploding face to face
Down its throat.

Can I also call you *Mount Gorrere*?
Where nobody escapes
Your choking them
With a thorn bush?

And can I call you *Mount Dibukh,*
Where you butchered the whole place?

Who's to say
What name I can use?
Now not even you.

What if I call you the
Mountain where we live?
I remember people begging,
"Help us up! Help us down!"

And the same people complaining,
"He's too strong! Too strong!"

Let them try
To take your place—at least, try!

anonymous
OUR STATE

Look at our state!
A fairyland of hate.
Dogs for guides,
Monkeys for guards,
A devil for a king,
His sister for a queen.
If we say a word,
They answer, "Shut up."

(. . .)*

Every office, every fief,
All the land and every life
Belong to them,
And we still pay
To dig our own graves.
The rage of God
Destroy this world—
But let us be saved.

---

* missing stanza

anonymous
SON AND FATHER

Father, I grieve as your son
As you pass from this world,
And I grieve as a poet.

I see you riding a mule,
Musket strapped to your shoulder—
No canes or staffs for you.

As you pass, a peasant cries:
I'm lost worse than my ox.

As you pass, a *mies** maker moans:
No more honey, no more honey.

As you pass, a priest asks:
Sanctuary? Where is my sanctuary?

I hear what you say:
Be generous, no other way.

Father, I grieve as your son
As you pass from this world.
I grieve as a wandering poet.

Let there be two of us
Making this journey.

---

* wine made from honey

NOTES ON TRANSLATIONS

Zeineb Yassin (1918–2005). "Under the Sycamores." Translation from Tigre with Dessale Berekhet. Veteran fighter in Eritrea's 30-year armed struggle for independence and mother of nine, Zeineb Yassin was popularly known as Mother Zeineb. "Under the Sycamores" is a transcription based on her performance on 1/15/2000 at the *Against All Odds* literary festival.

Saba Kidane (1978–). "War and a Woman." Translation from Tigrinya with Ghirmai Negash. Original taken from documentary film: *Against All Odds: African Languages and Literatures into the 21ˢᵗ Century.* Written and directed by Charles Cantalupo; produced by Audio Visual Institute of Eritrea (AVIE), Asmara; distributed by Michigan State University Press/African Books Collective: 2007.

Reesom Haile (1946–2003). "Angel Fiqriel," "Tell the President," "Her Picture," "One," "Jesus' Last Words," "African Anthem," "Eritrea's Daughter," "Poverty." Translations from Tigrinya with the author. A poet and scholar with a Ph.D. in Media & Communications from NYU, Reesom Haile is Eritrea's best known poet in the west. He returned to Eritrea in 1994 after an exile that included teaching and lecturing in western universities and working for international NGOs. His first collection of Tigrinya poetry, *Waza ms Qum Neger nTensae Hager* (Asmara: Francescana Printing, 1997), won the 1998 Raimok prize, Eritrea's highest prize for literature. His other books of poetry include *We Have Our Voice* (Trenton and Asmara: Red Sea Press, 2000; translations by Charles Cantalupo) and *We Invented the Wheel* (Trenton and Asmara: Red Sea Press, 2002; translations by Charles Cantalupo).

"What Can I Call You?" Translation from Tigrinya with Ghirmai Negash. Original untitled. An oral poet, Weldedingel, is believed to have composed the poem for a chief's funeral in the 1860s. Original taken from Ghirmai Negash, "Tigrinya Oral Poetry Recordings," curated in Leiden University, Department of Oriental Manuscripts & Printed Books (registration no. GB 1–24), 1995.

"Our State." Translation from Tigrinya with Ghirmai Negash. Original untitled. By anonymous oral poet. Original taken from Faïtlovitch, Jacques. *Giornale della Società Italiana* 23 (1911): 52–53.

"Son and Father." Translation from Tigrinya with Ghirmai Negash. Original untitled. By anonymous oral poet. Original taken from Faïtlovitch, Jacques. *Giornale della Società Italiana* 23 (1911): 50–51.

ACKNOWLEDGMENTS

The author gratefully acknowledges the previous publication of an earlier version of "Where War Was" in *Light the Lights* (Lawrenceville & Asmara: Red Sea Press, 2003) in which "Adulite" and "Poe in Massawa" also appeared. The author also gratefully acknowledges the previous publication of "Poe in Massawa" in *The Edgar Allan Poe Review* and in *Poe's Pervasive Influence* (Bethlehem and Lanham: Lehigh University Press/Rowman & Littlefield, 2012). Grateful acknowledgment of previous publications also includes: "Seeing Things" in *Titanic Operas*; "War and a Woman" in *UniVerse*; "Under the Sycamores," "African Leaders," "Angel Fiqriel," "Tell the President," "Her Picture," and "One" in *Per Contra*; "What Can I Call You" and "Son and Father" in *The Dirty Goat*; "Jesus' Last Words," "African Anthem," and "Poverty" in *Modern Poetry in Translation*. "African Anthem" also appears in *Centres of Cataclysm* (Bloodaxe Books, 2016). The author thanks the New York State Council for the Arts and City Lore for funding to work on the translations of "What Can I Call You?" "Our State," and "Son and Father." The author's gratitude for generous financial and in-kind support also extends to Eritrea's Research and Documentation Center (RDC), Cultural Affairs Bureau, and Penn State University's Schuylkill Campus (particularly the Office of Academic Affairs and the Office of University Relations), University College, Department of English, and College of Liberal Arts.

Printed in the United States
By Bookmasters